Mary Cohen

Christmas Quartetstart

Favourite carols arranged
for beginner string quartets

© 1999 by Faber Music Ltd
First published in 1999 by Faber Music Ltd
3 Queen Square London WC1N 3AU
Cover design by S & M Tucker
Music processed by Mary Cohen and Jackie Leigh
Printed in England by Halstan & Co Ltd

ISBN 0 571 51929 6

To buy Faber Music publications or to find out about the full range of titles
available please contact your local retailer or Faber Music sales enquiries:

Tel: +44 (0) 1279 82 89 82
Fax: +44 (0) 1279 82 89 83
E-mail: sales@fabermusic.co.uk
Website: http://www.fabermusic.co.uk

Contents

To the teacher

Christmas Quartetstart is designed for young players whose individual standard is about grade (AB) 1–2+ and who have some string quartet experience. Favourite carols and festive tunes are arranged in a wide variety of styles and textures – and in moods ranging from solemn and reflective to very boisterous – to provide ideal items for both carol services and school concerts. The rehearsal tips in the score are intended to be read out and discussed. Each individual part contains little technique tips throughout to help deal with problems which might otherwise disrupt the musical flow. 'Good King Wenceslas', 'Jingle Bells' and 'We wish you a merry Christmas' offer opportunities for audience participation, with sound effects, miming, shouts, *etc.*

Mary Cohen

Recommended background material

Mixed duet experience:
Superduets 1 for violin and cello (beginner)
Superduets 2 for violin and cello (established beginner – Grade 1)

Quartet experience:
Quartetstart Level 1 (Grade 1–2)
Quartetstart Level 2 (Grade 2–3)

All of the above titles are in Mary Cohen's **Superseries**
and are available from Faber Music.

Once in royal David's city

Henry John Gauntlett
(1805 – 76)

King's College, Cambridge has a famous tradition – they start their carol service with
a procession led by one chorister singing (unaccompanied) the first verse of this carol.

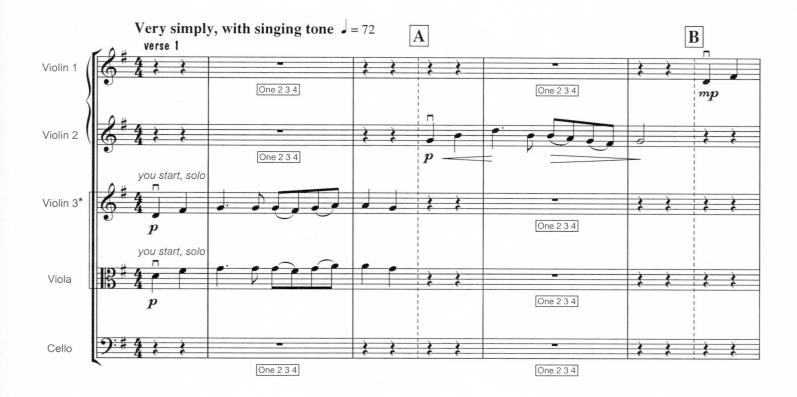

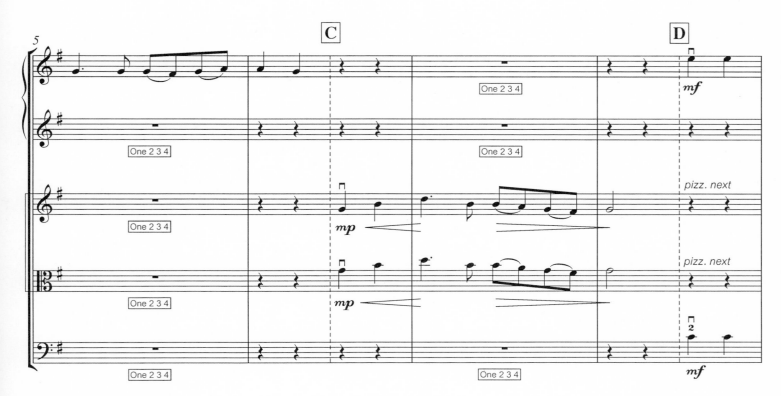

* Violin 3: alternative to Viola

© 1999 by Faber Music Ltd.

This music is copyright. Photocopying is illegal.

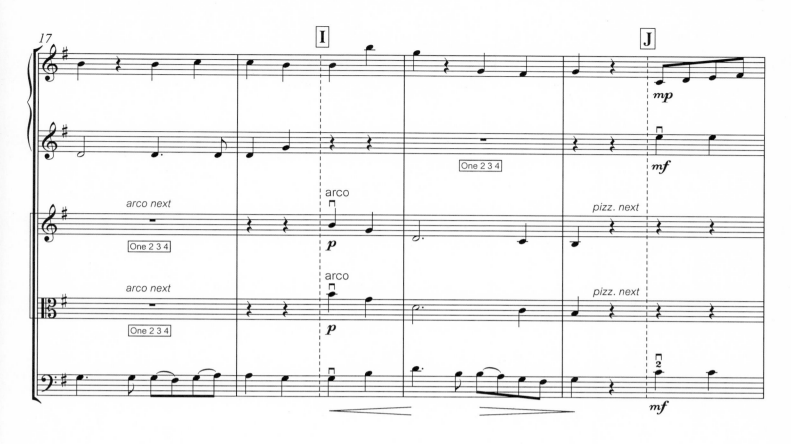

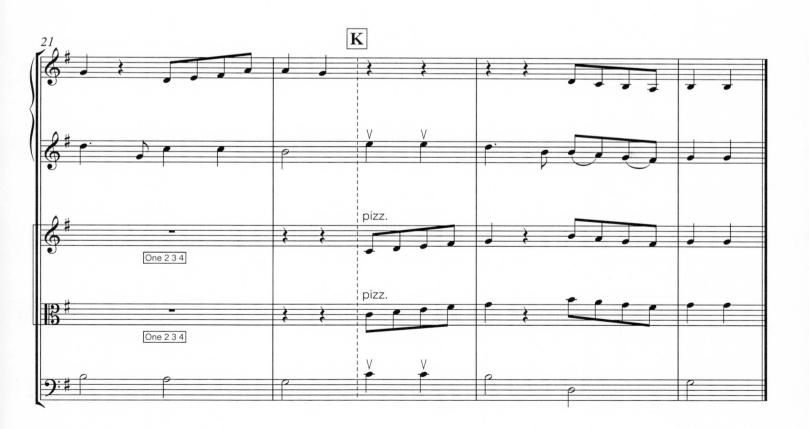

Good King Wenceslas

Fourteenth Century, Anon.

> Paint a scene in sound and actions with howling winds, clouds of snowflakes and King Wenceslas and his courtiers stamping the snow off their boots.

**Good King Wenceslas looked out on the feast of Stephen,
When the snow lay round about, deep and crisp and even.**

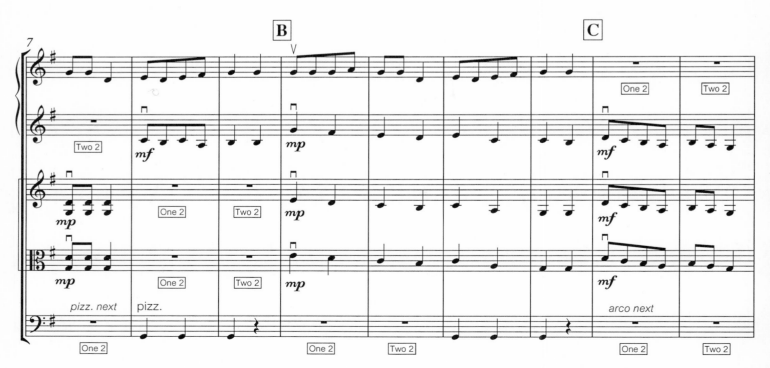

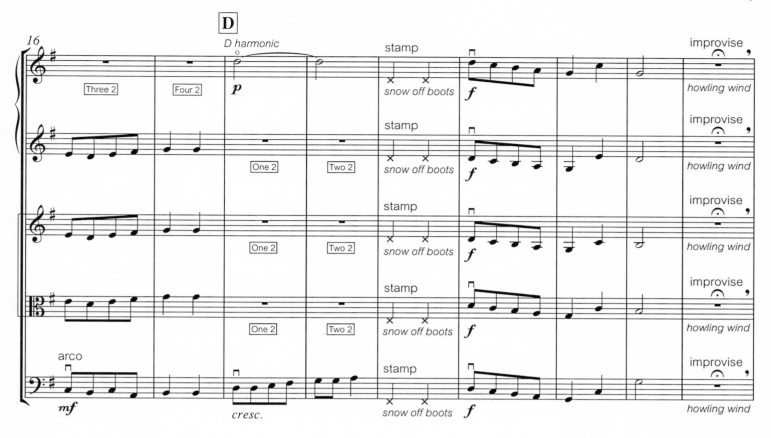

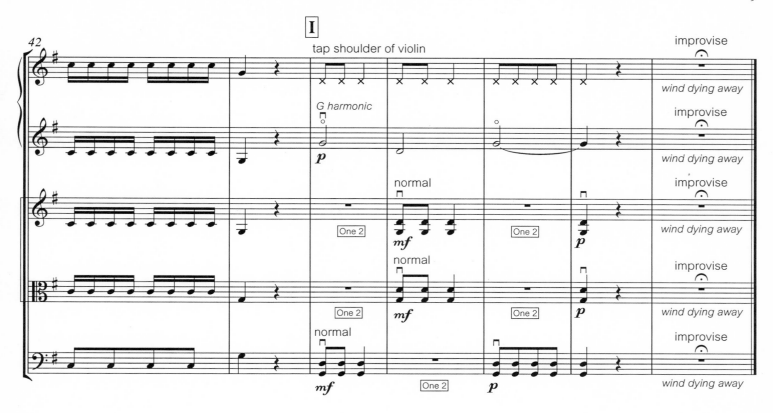

Away in a manger

William J. Kirkpatrick
(1838 – 1921)

Create a very calm atmosphere. Remember how famous artists of the past have painted the nativity scene – a dark stable with the central crib shimmering with light.

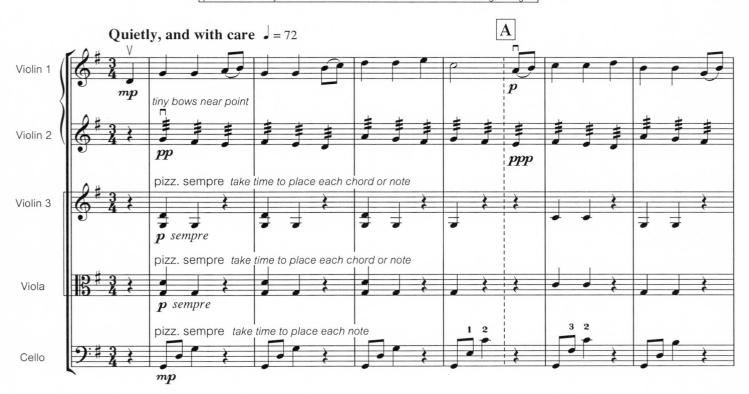

The Holly and the Ivy

English traditional

A lively, noisy scene: imagine a group of friends singing as they tramp through the woods to collect evergreens for Christmas decorations.

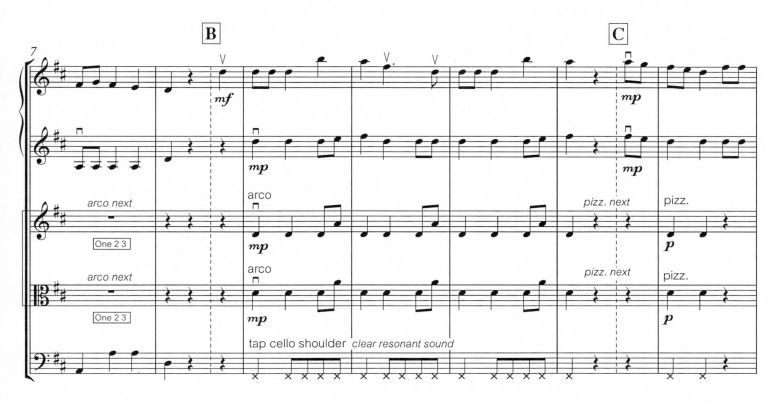

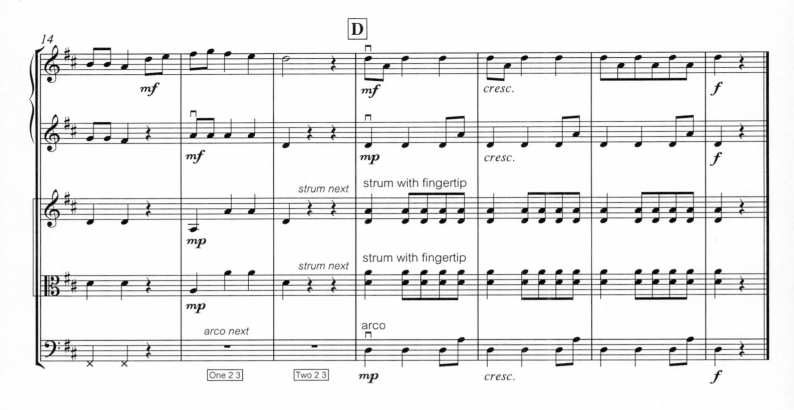

Silent night

Franz Gruber
(1787 – 1863)

6/8 needs to feel 'two-in-a-bar' all the way through. Practise clapping a few bars of each different rhythm, keeping the two ♩. beats with your foot.

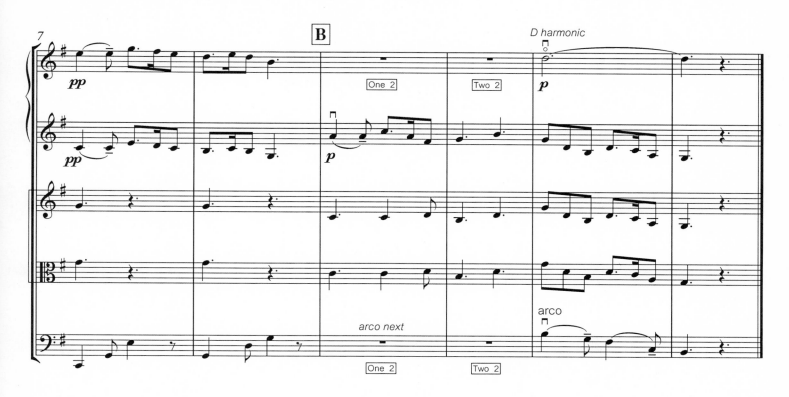

O come, all ye faithful

Anon.

This is the traditional Christmas Day hymn: imagine being inside a great cathedral singing along with the choir and organ, listening to bells pealing outside. Let bars 13 – 20 start quietly and build to a musical climax, but not too loud.

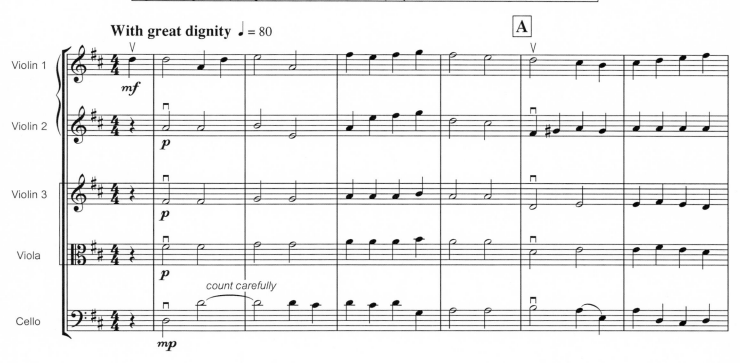

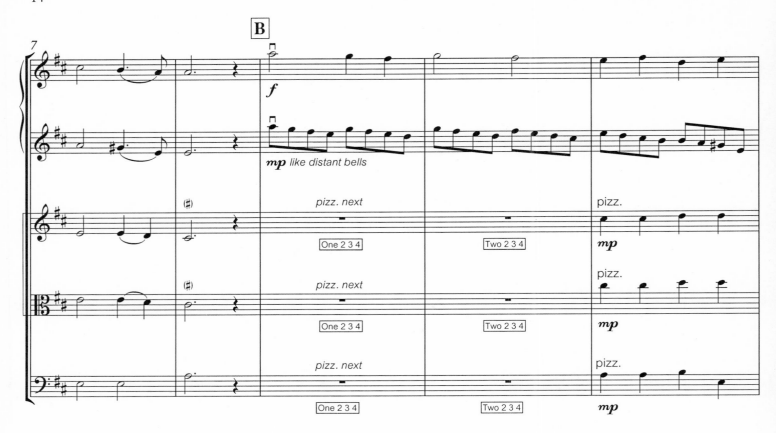

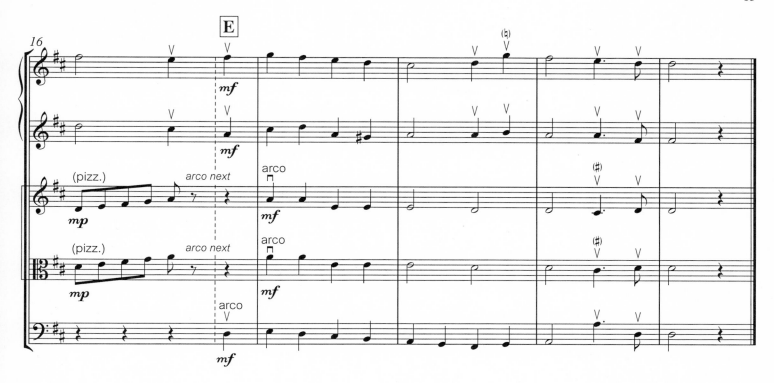

Jingle bells

James Pierpont
(1822 – 93)

A snowy Christmas card scene showing at least two horse-drawn sleighs. Experiment with staccato/spiccato bow strokes to find the best arco 'trotting' sound. The pizzicato 'trotting' passes from the cello to the viola/violin 3.

Trotting steadily along ♩ = 72

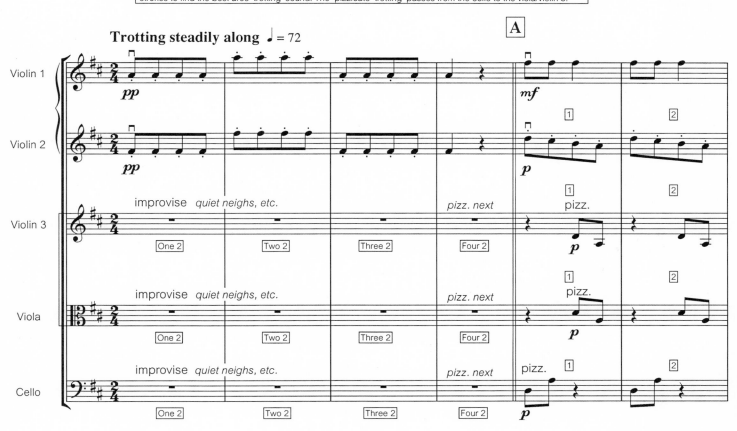

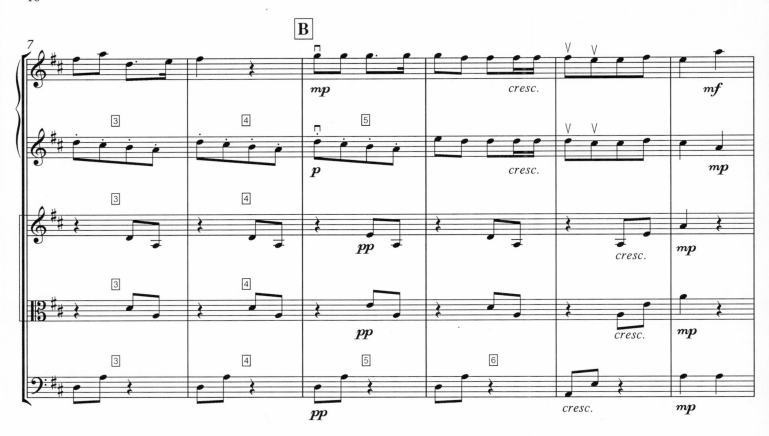

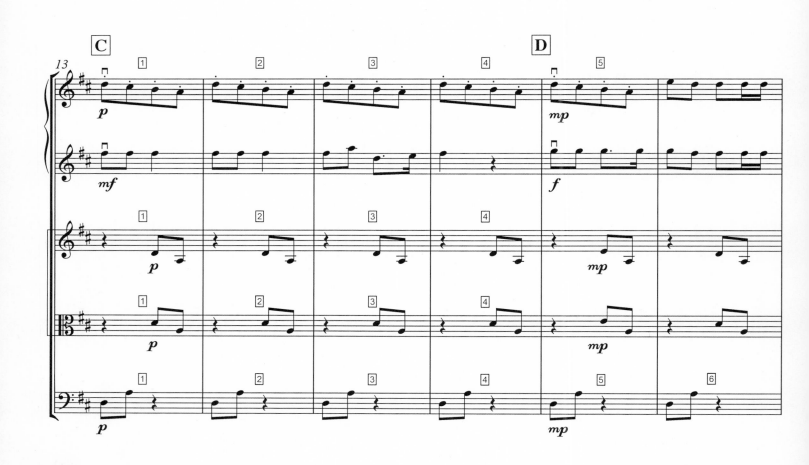

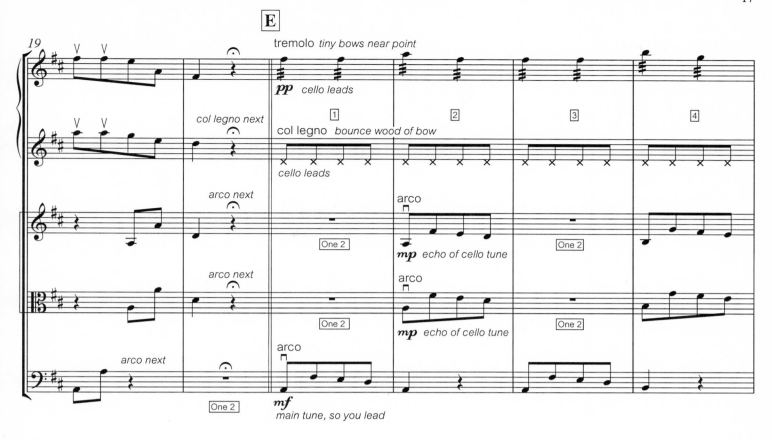

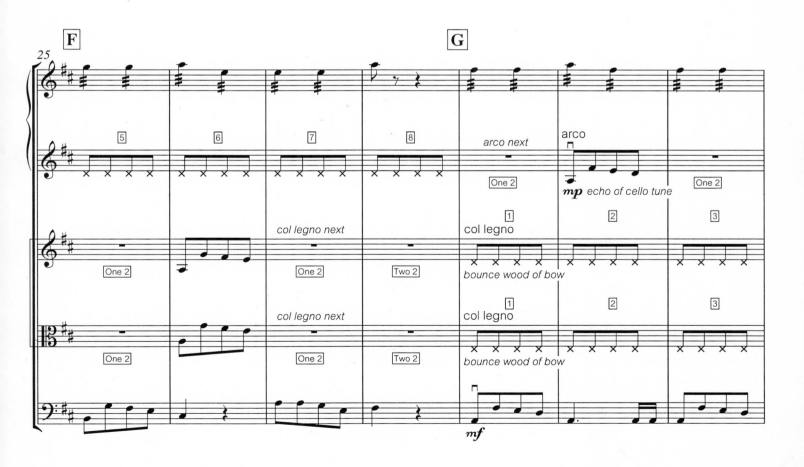

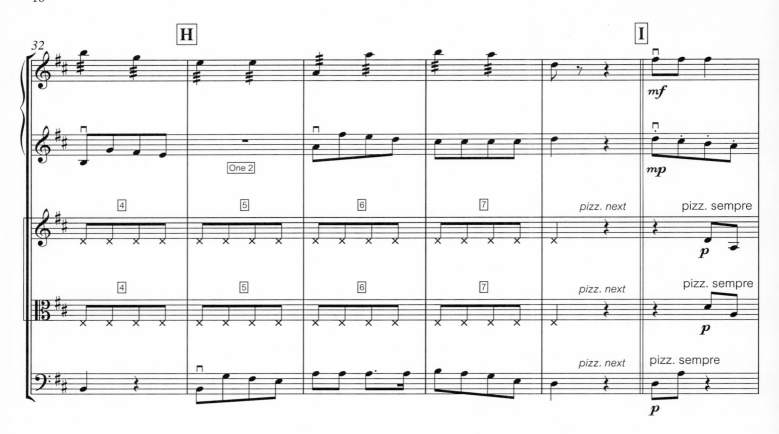

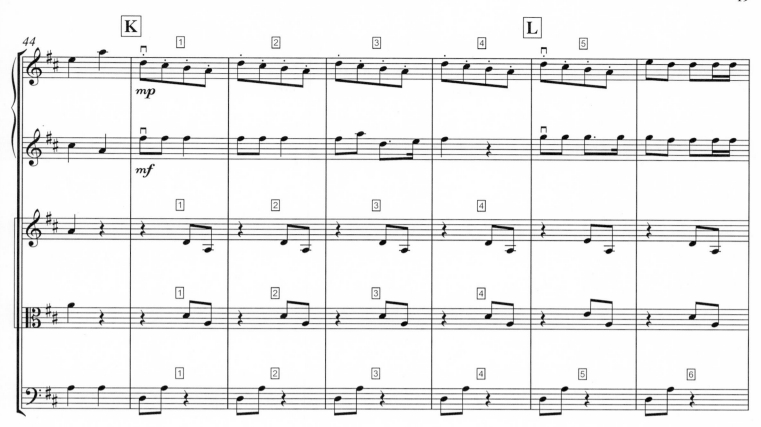

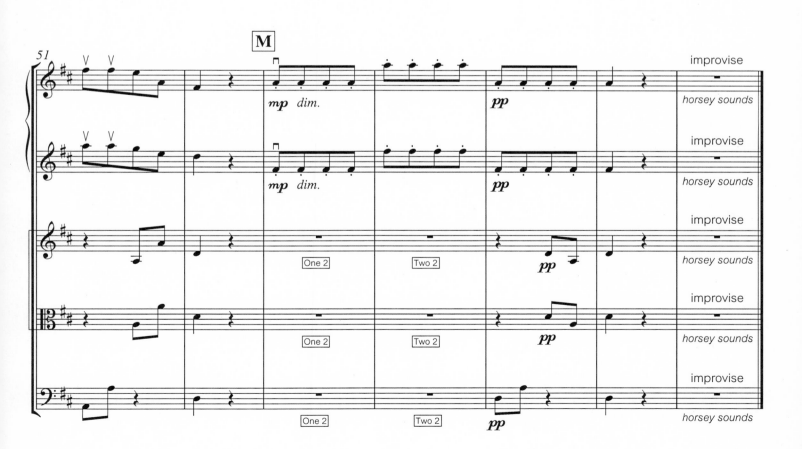

We wish you a merry Christmas

English traditional

A 'performance piece' which the audience may like to join in, either by singing the words of the carol or by making the noises and shouting! A group of carol singers is having a hard time with a Scrooge-like family who shout at them from an upstairs window. Set the scene with night-time sounds while the cellist is 'knocking' at the door.

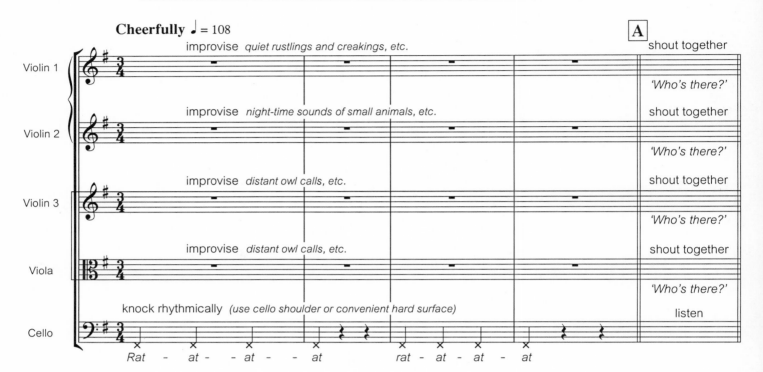

'We wish you a merry Christmas, we wish you a merry Christmas,
We wish you a merry Christmas and a happy New Year.
Good tidings we bring to you and your kin,
We wish you a merry Christmas and a happy New Year.'

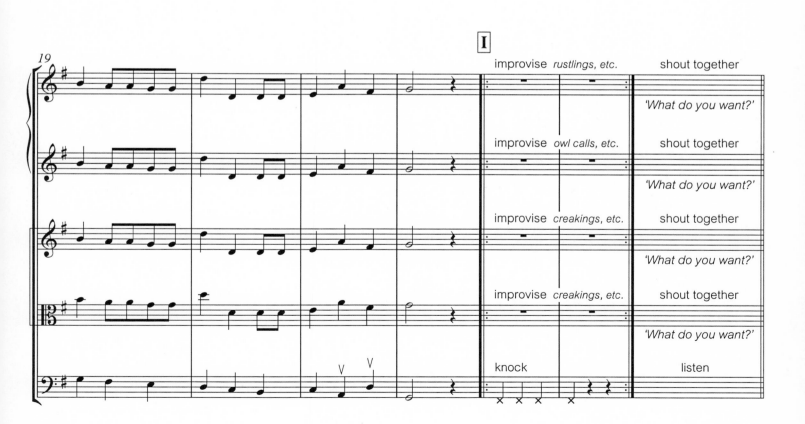

'Please bring us some figgy pudding', etc. ... 'and bring it out here.
Good tidings', etc.

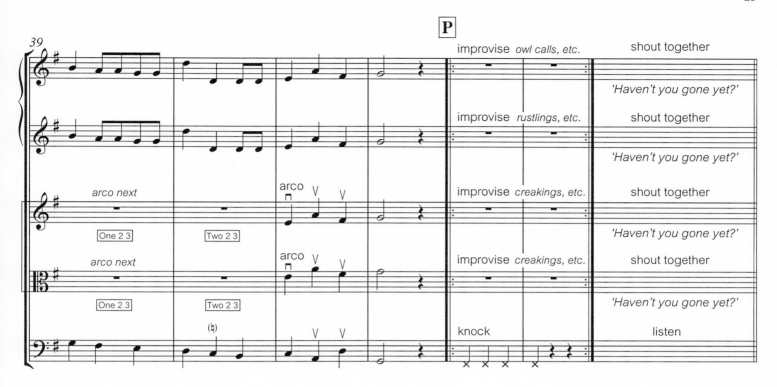

'We won't go until we've got some', etc. ... 'so bring some out here.
Good tidings', etc.

24

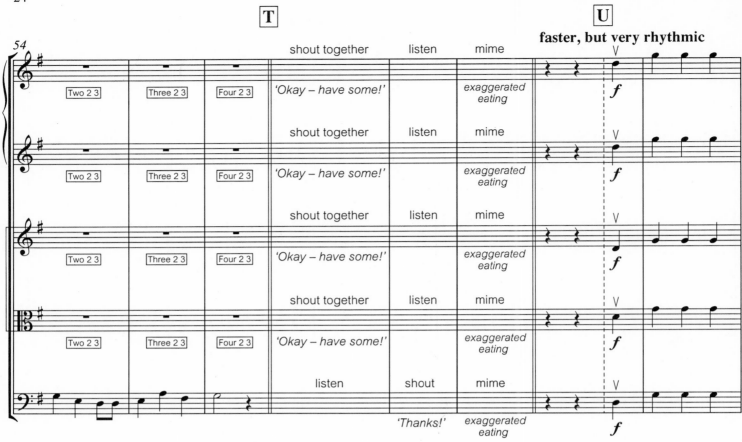

Reproduced and printed by
Halstan & Co. Ltd., Amersham, Bucks., England